wisecracks

wisecracks

everyday wit and wisdom

edited by tom burns

BARRON'S

First edition for North America published in 2005
by Barron's Educational Series, Inc.

First published in 2004 for
Whitcoulls Limited
61 Tidal Road
Mangere
Auckland
by Tangent Publications, an imprint of Axis Publishing Limited.

Copyright © 2004 Axis Publishing Ltd.

All inquiries should be addressed to:
Barron's Educational Series, Inc.
250 Wireless Boulevard
Hauppauge, New York 11788
www.barronseduc.com

Library of Congress Catalog Card No. 2004114881

International Standard Book No. 0-7641-5848-1

Conceived and created by
Axis Publishing Limited
8c Accommodation Road
London NW11 8ED
www.axispublishing.co.uk

Creative Director: Siân Keogh
Art Director: Clare Reynolds
Editorial Director: Anne Yelland
Production Controller: Jo Ryan

Printed and bound in China

9 8 7 6 5 4 3 2 1

about this book

Wisecracks brings together an inspirational selection of humorous phrases and sayings about life and the human condition, combined with evocative and gently amusing animal photographs that bring out the full comedy and pathos of human life.

A sense of humor is a vital antidote to today's stressful lifestyles. These humorous sayings will bring a smile to your face. These inspiring examples of wit and wisdom sum up the essence of the human world and its quirks and foibles.

about the author

Tom Burns is an editor and author who has been involved in publishing books and magazines across a wide variety of subjects for many years. From the many hundreds of contributions that were sent to him, he has selected the ones that are the wittiest and most quirky, and that best show how funny, bizarre, yet heartwarming life can be.

Tell a man there are 300 billion stars in the universe and he'll believe you. Tell him a bench has wet paint on it and he'll have to touch it to be sure.

A compromise is an agreement whereby both parties get what neither of them wanted.

Hospitality is making your guests feel at home…

…even if you wish they were.

It doesn't matter whether you win or lose…

…what matters is whether I win or lose.

Never wrestle with a pig.
You both get dirty and
the pig likes it.

Everyone has a photographic memory, but some people just don't have film.

Before you criticize someone,
walk a mile in his shoes.
That way, when you criticize him,
you're a mile away and
you have his shoes.

You don't leave room for pudding, you MAKE room.

Light travels faster than sound. This is why some people appear bright until you hear them speak.

They say that age
is all in your mind.
The trick is keeping
it from creeping
down into
your body.

A Freudian slip is
when you say one
thing but mean
your mother.

Exercise is a dirty
word. Every time I hear it,
I wash my mouth
out with chocolate.

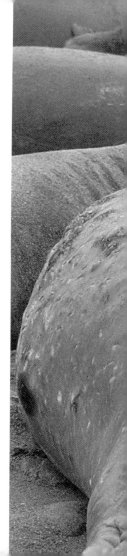

I intend to live forever;
so far, so good.

Without geography,
you're nowhere.

A New Year's resolution
is something that goes
in one year and
out the other.

In theory, there is no difference between theory and practice. But, in practice, there is.

The things that come to those who wait are usually the things left by those who got there first.

Tell me what you need,
and I'll tell you how to get
along without it.

I like deadlines, especially the whooshing sound they make as they fly by.

Things are more
like they are today
than they have
ever been before.

Always smile. It makes people wonder what you're up to.

Anything worth fighting for is worth fighting dirty for.

The sooner you
fall behind, the
more time you'll
have to catch up.

The most difficult part of attaining perfection is finding something to do for an encore.

Don't be irreplaceable.
If you can't be replaced,
you can't be promoted.

Anything worth doing is worth getting someone else to do.

Sincerity is the key. Once you can fake that, you've got it made.

A clear conscience
is usually the sign
of a bad memory.

Work fascinates me…

…I can sit and look
at it for hours.

I'm living so far beyond my income that we may almost be said to be living apart.

If you can keep your head while all around you are losing theirs, you probably don't understand the problem.

A father carries pictures where his money used to be.

Money talks—but all mine ever says is goodbye.

Therapy is expensive,
popping bubble wrap
is cheap…

…you choose!

Borrow money from pessimists—
they don't expect it back.

Christmas is the season when you buy this year's gifts with next year's money.

I started out with nothing and I still have most of it left.

If you think that something small can't make a difference, try going to sleep with a mosquito in the room.

By the time you can make ends meet, they move the ends.

A fine is a tax for doing wrong.

A tax is a fine for doing well.

Change is inevitable, except from a vending machine.

Today was a real
waste of makeup.

Home cooking: where
many a man thinks
his wife is.

Time is a circus—always packing up and moving on.

Women always worry about the things that men forget; men always worry about the things women remember.

Cleaning the house while your kids are growing up is like shoveling the path before it's stopped snowing.

If evolution has
progressed so far, how
come women only have
two hands?

When kids become wild and unruly, it is best to use a nice, safe playpen. Then when they're finished, you can just climb out.

Families are like fudge...

...mostly sweet with
a few nuts.

Family: a social unit where the father is concerned with parking space, the children with outer space, and the mother with closet space.

Boys will be boys,
and so will a lot of
middle-aged men.

Insanity is hereditary…

…you get it from your kids.

The trouble with being
a parent is that by the
time you are experienced,
you are unemployed.

The problem with the gene pool
is that there's no lifeguard.

I'm not 40…

…I'm 18 with 22 years' experience.

I like the 50-50-90 rule: anytime you have a 50-50 chance of getting something right, there's a 90 percent probability you'll get it wrong.

There are 10 types of people in the world. Those who understand binary and those who don't.

A recent survey shows
that three out of four
people make up
75 percent of the
world's population.

Research shows that
14 out of 10
people like chocolate.

42.7 percent of statistics
are made up on the spot.